Naked Lenses copyright 2017 © Careen Latoya Lawrence.

The author or authors assert their moral right under the Copyright, Designs and Patents Act, 1988, to be identified as the author or authors of this work.

All Rights reserved. No part of this publication may be reproduced, copied, stored in a retrieval system, or transmitted, in any form or by any means, without the prior written consent of the copyright holder, nor be otherwise circulated in any form of binding or cover other than that in which it is published and without a similar condition being imposed on the subsequent purchaser.

A CIP catalogue record for this title is available from the British Library.

ISBN 978-1-5272-1513-9

www.CareenLatoya.com

Acknowledgement

To say this book was easy to compile would be an understatement. It has taken me months to finalise ideas and I have had some extremely patient friends by my side. I would like to thank five lovely ladies in particular. They have all gone through my turbulent mind-set with me, some more than others and they have all stuck by my side and supported me, more than they even know. I couldn't have asked for much better friends. So, a huge thank you goes to Laurie-Ann Brown, Roberta Collier, Alicia Duncanson, Rosie Fennell, and Ellenor McIntosh.

I extend my thanks to the *Words Down* writing group who have been positively critical of some of the pieces that I would be able to dismantle them and recreate them to the standard you have before you to be enjoyed for breakfast, lunch and dinner. Another thank you goes to my friend Olivia Newnham who has also been a shining star, helping me to finalise the edits of this book. You my dear Olivia, are fantastic. Being able to go through the poems you went through in such a tight tight frame was, to me, outstanding and I do appreciate it. Not forgetting the outstanding poet Emmanuel Sugo. I'd like to thank you ever so much for the time you have taken within your busy schedule to have a look through some of these pieces for me, even inspiring one as well.

I could not ever leave my parents out of my thanks: my father, Courtney, and mother, Hazeline Lawrence. I would not have started writing had it not been for them. The little chatterbox in me led them to encouraging me to write my thoughts down and introducing me to the wonderful world of books from an exceptionally young age. Had I not started there, I would not be where I am today.

Before my final thanks, I must mention Poetic Unity where I was able to test out many of my pieces at the weekly event held at the Black Cultural Archives in Brixton. Just to be able to share the pieces and hear them back has helped me with doing my editing when listening back to them. The platform offered by Poetic Unity definitely helps with the writing process as it does the performing.

My final thanks must go to the men who have inspired me along this journey. These stories are largely inspired by the men I have crossed paths with. Many of them being worn on their bones, some shared through their conversations, others a result of their actions based on society's definition of how they should present themselves and what they are to mean to women.

Introduction

When I set out on this journey, I had no idea what I was to expect from myself. I knew I wanted to write about my experiences being single, but, wasn't entirely sure how I would go about doing it. I danced through a mountain of ideas and found I couldn't settle on one. It wasn't until the first poem about Mr. 181 before I realised what this mission was to be about.

I then figured that writing about being single across numerous pages was not the route for me to take. It was bigger than a relationship segment which possibly belonged in a magazine. This book was about seeing men through clear eyes without being tainted with any form of self-pity or pressures from society about being 27 and single.

This journey has been exciting, scary, tiring, and most of all, satisfying. I am pleased with the work I have produced and honestly do hope you enjoy it. I hope that at least one of these poems will resonate deeply within you, as some of them have already done within the hearts of audiences who received them. I hope to empower, inspire and motivate you as you turn the pages of this book.

While writing this book, and attending open mic nights and performing on other platforms, I have taken away many lessons. However, the lesson I have become stuck with is one to accept perfection as an element of perseverance. I share this with you because I want you to persevere in all you do, for that is the only way you will find perfect peace in satisfaction.

Contents

1 of 13	8
Naked Lenses	9
Russel Square Gardens	10
Ned	11
To Be	13
2 of 13	14
Peacefully Caged	15
Nine Letters	17
The One	21
Two Little Soldiers	24
3 of 13	27
Mr. Adidas	28
Street Art	29
Young Boys	31
Young Short Man	32
4 of 13	33
Young Crystal Ball	34
Young Restless	35
Young Menace	36
Young Him Against Me	37
5 of 13	38
The Young Newbie	39
Young Boy or Man	40
Father's Love	41
Omari	42
6 of 13	45
Mr. With Your Pain	46
Mr. Archer	48
Mr. Unknown	49
The Underground	50
7 of 13	51
Instigated Freestyle	52
Secret Souls	54

Mr. 181	55
My Stranger	56
8 of 13	58
Mr. Jubilee Line	59
Danger	62
Mr. Where is Home?	65
Mr. Forgotten	67
9 of 13	68
Mr. Middle East	69
Mr. Grey	71
Mr. Poetry Luv	73
Mr. Swag	75
10 of 13	78
My Mind Her Body	79
Taxi Thugs	83
The Train Fella	85
Black King	87
11 of 13	90
Dear White Boy	91
Mr. 8-8:40pm	93
Seek Ye First	95
App	98
12 of 13	102
Mr's Call Girl	103
10 for Me	107
Mr. You	109
Mr. Suleiman	114
13 of 13	116
Friday's King	117
Mr Please-Call-Me	120
it was LOVE	122
Find Your Voice	125
Cherry Blossom	**128**

Inhale the surrounding peacefulness, that you will accept the turbulences to come. Inhale the surrounding joy, that your heart will be at ease when the storms rise.

Inhale love, that you will give it to others in their time of need. Rise with the sun as it looks over the Earth.

-Careen Latoya-

Naked Lenses

It surprises me that I feel this way.
Mountains of security crashing down,
With waves of streaming thoughts
Rolling through windows of my opened soul.

Awkwardly cowering from given opportunities I've
drawn attention to my nakedness,
Shining in the shadows of the dimmed moonlight.
Mellow dramatic themes playing the intro to *'My
Heart's Sorrow'*.

Hunny, I do miss you.
Accept my apology for leaving you
Now I have a nagging uncomfortable feeling
As though I've done something wrong.

But I know exactly where you are.
Close to a central location.
Naked, open, and waiting to be held.
Trying to preserve your energy
For our connection to be felt.

I bought you so we could
Begin a partnership.
Yet I've abandoned you.
Taking time for myself.
Now I've no videos
Or pictures as proof
Of the fantastic night
We should have enjoyed

Russell Square Gardens

He swims in bodies of beings
who have come to engross themselves
in the blessings handed to him by Mother Nature.

He satisfies them,
Displaying Mother Nature's love,
As they laugh with each other.

Breath-taking moments are captured.
Bodies shudder.
Teaching eyes to peacefully gain his beauty.

Allowing them to dance over his pavements,
He encases them in warmth;
Creating a sense of security for them.

He is perfect for many.
The master of escapism.
The author of peace.

Kind in many ways.
Never shirking
from their unbearable pains.

Knowing exactly where to guide their hearts; When they cry,
as he knows every corner of his home.

He, Russell, identifies with them,
swims in their bodies,
guiding them as their feet make connections with him.

Ned

I'm grateful for the father I have
And I know your parenting skills
Were not found on the pages of self-help books.

I love you.

Sometimes we forget the meaning
Of the most difficult phrase
We could ever come across.

You've always preferred
Our love to be shown
As opposed to simply sliding through parted lips.

A father.

You are to my sister and I.
Though we are far from perfect,
You nurtured us to be two beautiful young women.

A husband.

For twenty-eight years
You knew forever was the life
You wanted with our mother.

Ned.

The name you are called
As 'dad' has been abolished
But you don't mind, for all you want is our respect.

My first love.

From the way you've treated mom
To the conversations you've had with me To
teach me what love is all about.

With all my heart
I thank you for everything
As without you, I wouldn't be who I am today.

Happy birthday boss.

By the way,
How old are you again?

To Be

Father to be,
There are no nine-month crash courses
To teach you to be the 'World's Best Dad'.
It's your judgement that will guide you
And there are many years ahead
In need of lessons per hour
For your child
To present experiences yet to be written about.

Father to be,
No matter how conscientious you are now,
There will be days your efforts will be futile
And your mind will ask to be shut off.
But you can't give up when life gets difficult
For your child ought to learn how to overcome adversities.
The cloak of strength you received
Is to be shared with the generation you created
To have an eternity.

Father to be,
Supersede society's expectation.
Be the superhero your child needs.
Become the example you've always hoped for.
Learn the lessons you are to teach.
Use your experiences to help you.
For there are no nine-month crash courses
To teach you to be 'World's Best Dad'.

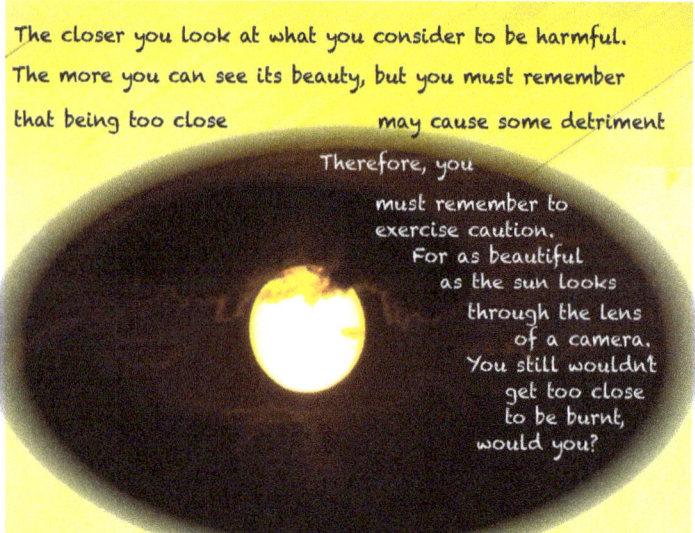

The closer you look at what you consider to be harmful. The more you can see its beauty, but you must remember that being too close may cause some detriment Therefore, you must remember to exercise caution. For as beautiful as the sun looks through the lens of a camera. You still wouldn't get too close to be burnt, would you?

- Careen Latoya -

Peacefully Caged

Peace resides in a nest
unscrupulously formed
by hearts of dreary saints

Lyrically
stepping
  on
untainted
leaves

Leaving the rest of us with hazy eyes
Unable to see the beauty in this malicious world
Stepping aside wondering...

With pins pricking our every being
We become
                              ALL SEEING
Visualising nothing.
As the world waits with unending time
Wanting scales to
                Fall
                From
                Our

                Eyes

For us to experience the tranquillity in
This distraught creation.

But we are so hung up on
Trying to find the
Nestled peace
Hidden in unfathomable depths

And forgetting to enjoy the beauty
Given to us by clean hands.

                                                                Always apologetic
                        Begotten by broken
            Cold cisterns.

Despicable.

But why must you apologise for your happiness?
Smile away your pains
Wave goodbye to yester-folks
For they are just jester-yokes
Wanting you to be bound
To their oppressive ways
As they dismiss your every thoughts
Forcing you to feel

                                        h o l l o w.

Start anew
Look around you
Experiencing
the small prints
As you turn a new page everyday.

Find the friends who remind you of your worth
Tell your family you love them
Tap into your creativity
Find true peace
For its suppression
Is a product of your repression
On a painting handed to you at birth.

But,
Do you know you're too strong to be held down
And are as free as a bird in its cage.

Nine Letters

    You are:
Adjusted by labels,
Defined by materials,
Trapped in misunderstandings.
Nine letters long
Three syllables short.

    You are:
Unfound in pictures,
Hidden in movies,
Ridiculed in songs.
Nine letters long
Three syllables short.

    You are:
Afraid of yourself,
Redefined by numbers,
Barely alive where you stand.
Nine letters long
Three syllables short.

You say you are, <u>b</u>roken
              <u>e</u>ndangered
              <u>a</u>ngered
              <u>u</u>nknown
              <u>t</u>ough
              <u>i</u>ndecent
              <u>f</u>oul
              <u>u</u>gly
              <u>l</u>ivid

But to me you are:
Beautiful.
Not only nine letters long and
Three syllables short.

Yet the world tells you
You are too fat to fit
In the box they created
Which has no adjustable straps.
Wanting you to change
So you will be just like them.

Always having to compete
Because your skin doesn't match
And minds are so closed.
They are afraid because
You to them are to be extinct.

Wondering what life would be like
If only you weren't here
Forced to think you were God's mistake
Because you've been 'patched' together
With different islands upon your skin.
Why are you not whole in tone?

    You are,
On your own
Learning to appreciate you
Trying to find similarities
So you can present it to them
That they will hopefully accept you,

    You are,
Self-destructive
Because no-one's spotted you
No-one knew the truth
Of the internal wars
You've been forced to battle.

    You are,
Looking for a hero
For you haven't identified the hero in you

And you've forgotten the
"I LOVE YOU'S"
From the lips of your parents
As you've put them down to be
liars.

Will you allow me
To help to redefine you?
For you are,
      Brave
       Encouraging
      Ambitious
       Understanding
       Trustworthy
      Industrious
      Faithful
       Unshakeable
      Life.

You are,
The giraffe amongst them all,
Able to view the world from above
As they struggle to be comfortable in your skin.
They shudder in your presence
Brains hardwired to jeer
Stirring from your strength
Shaking their core with discomfort.

You are,
    Brightly shining.
    Entertaining continuously.
    Accentuating perfected flaws.
    Undeniably determined.

Taunting taints.
Irrefutably fighting.
Flying high above the abuse.
Upcycling negativity.

Loosening words from mental grips.

You are,
A superhero,
Saving the lives of those
Who feel as though they too are
The world's flavour of ugly.

Your poise,
The grace you carry,
Your elegance,
The tender words you utter,
Your belief in yourself,
Stands out in crowds of unwavering souls.

You
Adjust labels
Define materials
Escape misunderstandings

You are
More than
9 letters long
And 3 syllables short.

You are:
Eloquently beautiful.

The One

She is the one who
                Cares enough to fight.
                No-one else understands
                Yet everyone wants to suggest
                What she should do
                And how it should be done.

She is the one who
                Cries frustrated tears,
                With voices telling her to pack it in
                As fingers point
                And judgements are cast
                Shoving depression on her back.

She is the one who
                Loves hard enough,
                Refusing to give up
                Though those in the system
                Are quick to turn away.

Why should they love as much
When the child is not theirs?

She is the one who
                Carried him for nine months
                Nurturing him to this day.
                Travelling on public transport
                Hoping he sits for the next two
                stops.

She is the one.
                The mother who struggles alone.

> Learning more about her son as he grows,
> Praying he does not fall into the wrong crowd
> Hoping he makes it through the system he was forced into.

But the ignorance of many
Fails him over and over again.

She is the one who
> Manages his meltdowns
> And the tantrums he throws
> Because it's all too much.
> He's unable to say how he feels
> And now, she's at the end of her road.

She is the mother of a child,
A son, who the world gave up on.
Forced to fight
For the perfect provisions.
One to suit his needs
To grant him the education she can't provide.

He is the son who,
Has autism,
ASD as it is shortened,
Poor home training, they've called it
A bad mother, she is labelled.
He is the one whom
They look at and assume
He is a 'typically developed' kid
So forget he needs support.
Forgetting he even requires patience
With what we class as simple.

He, is her son.
Someone else's child
Whom I have enjoyed working with. The one who taught me patience And how to be a child again.

Two Little Soldiers

I - Introduction

Two little soldiers were brought together by God.
He chose their mother,
And reshaped her heart
He fastened them with strength
For life would take a wrong turn,
Or so it may have seemed then
As she now shows no sign of regret.

She draws strength from her soldiers
Who take turns to refuel her.
Non-stop mother.
These trips, recurring, as short and as long as they feel
She continues for them.

Brave little soldiers.
Men after her own heart.
She follows their lead,
Draws strength from their strength
Even amid her tired, exhausted, anxiety ridden state.

II - Archie

You little soldier,
Your brother loves you,
He grows weary when he does not see you.
The nights you spend in that hospital bed, he becomes restless
Wrestling nerves,
Wanting you to be with him
Or him with you.

He wants things to be normal,
But he knows it is not always possible
And he continues to treat you as best as he can.
Running out of words,
His energy is hyperactive.

Putting a spring into him when he gets to visit you
Laying awake for as long as able.
He may be having troubles when you are not around
Where he'd have been able to sleep soundly knowing
You are at home with him.

III - Reggie

God created you as a pair of soldiers
For one without the other would struggle.
So, SON,
Please understand
You are here to keep your brother's head held high.
Cry with him in secret when mother is not watching over your shoulders
And listen to the hum of his heart.

He loves you as much as you do him.
Maybe even more,
But you are here to fight with each other.
To keep each other active.
To help mother to keep moving.

You have been patient with life,

Knowing he could have been born without an illness,
Waiting for his recovery,
And tolerant, though it may be taking much longer than you'd have wished for.

IV - Conclusion

Two little soldiers
As brave as those fighting wars for this great country,
I admire your loving bond
And the embraces you give to your mother who does all she can to stand for you.

You keep her on her toes
Obligingly,
That she may not yield to defeat
And love drives your actions
Reminding her what it means to be strong.

Brave little soldiers,
Created by God,
Holds each other
Wiping the tears from mother's eyes
Whispering into her ears that you love her
Being the backbone for each other
Knowing you without the other would be a lonely atom.

Allow yourself to sink into the stillness as your body sculpts itself to be moulded and become one with your environment. Take the time as the sun rises to let your pains melt away into the darkness of last night.

- Careen Latoya -

Mr Adidas

Caramel has been drizzled over your smooth skin
Infused with your stubble from this morning's shave.

Your voice, its huskiness
Latches onto my ears, wrapping itself around me.

Mr Adidas,
You're admirable to me,

Not only are you a handsome painting
But your sense of self is appealing.

The authority you exert
Causes them to respect you.

You've got the right methods
And they know your expectations.

It's the military stance you have
Which calls for the respect you gain.

Now I wish
Others would be more like you.

Street Art

It may drive them to insanity
But gives you peace of mind

It may force them to hide
But pushes you to be bold

Follow the art to reconnect
Follow the art to find a heart.

I ventured out of my comfort zone
From the sounds of strings
Wishing to embrace the many
Who hoped to be soothed.

My best friend
Gave me the courage
To fear nothing and
Dared me to be bold.

There, I met Street Art.
Up close and personal
Giving me lessons in history,
Explaining the ways of this current world.

Laying out his art against war
He was willing for his work to be captured
Just as long as something was bought
All to support the cause.

People, he spoke,
Are no longer seeking change
For 9/11 scared them
It stole their courage

Now, wars, he continued
Are used as a distracting force
Taking our thoughts away from the truth
'It's now time we take a stand'.

He described the 80s as a vibrant place,
No-one would have stepped down
When voices were to be heard.
Injustices were fought, for the importance of lives.

He was the Street Art that carved words into hearts
On the sidewalks of Shoreditch High Street.
Supporting movements unseen
Speaking volumes for those who are hurting.

Young Boys

They are our boys.
And we know those we expect to fail.
And whether they understand the importance of now,
We will never know.

We have spoken enough
Tried hard enough
But somehow the responses we receive
Distances them from our efforts.

They leave us with questions
We no longer ask
For they have forced us to give up
Tying our hands behind our backs.

There will no longer be
A future generation
If their will to achieve has died.

They should not fail
But idiocy and pride entertains their minds
So attempt to look good for friends
Becoming labels and stereotypes.

Young Short Man

Living up to stereotypes
Already attached to him.
He acts like the 'man',
Just to be seen and heard.

I wonder if he knows
How stupid this is?
He is another smart one,
With no self-respect.

Throwing his life away
Disregarding the help given to him
Losing connections to keep him grounded

I wish life would give him a sign,
To show him what this route has lined up for him
Hoping it will mean something to him.

There will be moments where it is difficult to stand and face your problems
And there is nothing wrong with lifting your feet from their planted positions
To go the other way to seek something better.
The grass isn't greener on the other side,
But you can, without a doubt, tend to a new land which is barren
That one day it will be fruitful.

-Careen Latoya-

Young Crystal Ball

He is unseen to all
Lost in the crowds
Just another wannabe
Acting like the rest

He awaits his time to come
To be captured by the life
Lost his identity
Puffing up his chest

I've looked into the crystal ball
Hurt by what I have seen.
He will be another 'one of them'
If he stays where he is.

The wrong crowds will have sucked him in
If he refuses to remove himself
He doesn't seem to identify
Those in this establishment
Willing to help him.

It is an unfortunate case
This generation has become blind
They would prefer to do things their way
Unaware they may become another number in the system.

Young Restless

He once told me
Of a future for himself.
But now it's hard to believe
The sincerity I heard.

His words were clear
Danced gracefully across the empty space
Landing lightly in my cerebrum
That they could be processed and logged well.

Now I can't understand
What caused his dream to die.
His self-belief now inexistent
He now slowly floats through life.

He no longer cares,
Masking that he once did.
Stopped presenting himself well
Constantly defying authority.

The wind takes him down dark alleys
Where he seemed to have lost his way.
I've always tried to help
But the end for me is near.

Young Menace

He smiles that sinister smile
Time and time again
Hoping for a reaction
Time and time again.

He no longer cares
And ensures we all know
Unleashing his torment
Time and time again.

His friends are just like him
All showing no ambition showing.
Constantly join his mockery
Time and time again.

He enjoys his misfortunes
Aware of his stupidity
Trying to prove to be brainless
Time and time again.

His mother expects nothing better from him
Time and time again.
It is difficult to get through to a kid like him
Time and time again.

Young Him Against Me

I once had faith in him,
Against all odds
He seemed to understand life
And he was, well, is smart.

The only issue then and now
Was the same thing,
He just like the menace,
Hates authority.

Demanding the respect he believes he is owed
Refusing to give it to those in power
Believing they do not deserve it
And his wrongs find an alibi in his excuses

It's as though he believes
The world owes him something
Skipping through life's lanes
Doing that which his heart desires.

Now I feel I'm not being paid
Enough to deal with abuse from kids
Yet he gives it to me
And gives it to me hard.

My body is drained of its energy.
I'm close to giving up.
But as the days go by
I remember my end is much closer.

Follow the path
The path which made you the happiest,
The path which holds comfort closely,
The path which has been your security.
Follow the path you know will lead you to success.
Do not stray from it.

-Careen Latoya-

The Young Newbie

He started,
I gave the same talk
Hoping he would be inspired.

Spoke about being here
And what would happen
If he failed his six weeks trial

He had plans lined up for the future
And I believed him
Not quite like the others who no longer care

Time to time he'd get into problems
But I still believe in him
For he still has his flame.

Young Boy or Man

He could have a better future
But something about him,
Something deeper needs to be challenged.

He's a smart boy,
But has seemingly been misguided,
Having chosen the wrong crowd.

It would be a shame
To see his life fall through the drains.
But if he wants nothing for himself,
Well, that's an empty jar to fill.

I wish he could see himself.
See himself through our eyes
But also through his own
For he needs to learn that lesson.

A boy should not be a grown man
If he has nothing to build a home.
A boy should not be a grown man,
If he has no respect for himself or life.

Father's Love

How much longer will you cradle your dissatisfaction,
Nurturing its developments to tear you apart?
Can you not see how hostile you've become?

Your composition is no longer the same.
Instability plagues your thoughts.
Your words, now openly soiled

You are unable to look past the pain
To find the love he has for you.
Do you still resent him?

Your father that is?
Have you forgotten all he's done for you?
Do you still hug tightly your hatred for him?

You've had the fatherly love many crave
Yet you've dismissed it,
Struggling to smile a second time.

As the sun sets in the west
So should your pain.
Allow it to put your restlessness to bed.

Omari

I looked Life in his eyes
And there you were,
Breathing without a care in the world,
Eyes closed as Life held your hand,
Caught up in Time
As Time stood still,
I was there.

You were resting.
Your Soul, visible,
Spoke silently to me
Yet your voice was withheld
Deep within a tomb of brokenness.
We were peaceful
And you floated in an ocean of tranquillity.

Flowers to your left
The window, path for escape
Also to your left.
But you laid there.
Still.
We had the place to ourselves
Chaperoned by Time, Life and Soul.

Your Soul wounded by a bullet
Incomprehensibly strung pain within me
Forcing us together,
As Fear rode its way through loved ones,
Yours.
My time with you was brief,

You told me you would be okay;
Through closed eyes,
Lips unmoving,
Messages sent through Soul.
I stood by your bed,
Held your hand in mine,
You told me to let the rest know you'd be fine.
I believed you weren't going anywhere
Because you said so.

We communicated.
I was there.
Long enough to feel you.
Long enough to see you.
Long enough to share with you.

A 10-hour journey
Took seconds.

Legs crossed,
Sitting under the moonlight
Which shun through
The diamond crossed windows
Of my parents' room,
My laptop opened,
Trying to get the latest about you

Yet,
None of it was required.

I was transported to you.
I saw you
And it was as real as me
Aged 18,
On the floor of my parents' room
And I delivered your message,
And couldn't keep to myself that,
I was with you.
I stood there and watched you.
You told me not to worry.
You,
You used your Soul to speak to me.
You were not conscious but I heard you.

When the silence gets too loud,
Embark on a journey which allows you to escape in structures
Closing your mind from the solidarity that's spiralled out of control.

-Careen Latoya-

Mr With Your Pain

The perplexed look on your face
Breeds concern in me

Now you've become a troubled picture
With a tightly knitted jaw
Painted on the forefront of my memory.

Your caged anger perspires
As you ponder.
I do wish I could read minds.

Your lowered eyes
Bears a striking resemblance
To a grieving widow.

Hypnotising me.
Now shredded evidence of your distress
Falls as snow into the lap of my heart.

Time's cold chill
Wormed its way
Through to your tightly knitted jaw

Lingering on my closed lids.
More than twenty-four hours later
I can still see you fighting tears

As they drown and consume you.
Mr With Your Pain,
What could I have done to help you?

I wish I reached out to touch you
But its inappropriacy
Would have stirred an uncomfortable dust.

The cloak of despair you wore
Tugged at my heart
Telling me you needed a shoulder to lean on

But fear stopped me from asking

Mr Archer

> *Sex sells,*
> *But it kills the seller.*

I knew a little about this man
But not enough to understand
Why his voice was lost
In a space left open as years.
As I watched his video
I tried to search his eyes for clues
That would prove the discomfort.

I guess it gets easier to wear a poker face
With directors and editors hiding the
Mask of uncertainty from us.
However, that doesn't really matter
When that which is demanded by the money holders
Is a body which 'every' woman wants to be on top of hers.

When did it become okay for an individual,
To be demeaned and sexually distraught?
Women constantly complain about being used as sex objects
Yet we forget that men also have the same rights.
So why should we put pressure on them
To satisfy our sexually impoverished minds?

Yes. His body is perfect, but is it fair
For anyone to ask him to strip
And undress for the women of the world
To salivate over him and crave his presence at night?
Is he not good enough to entertain us vocally
Instead of destroying him psychologically
And push him into drugs and alcoholism?

Mr Unknown

I'm finding it difficult to identify the colour of your hair
I can see the streaks of grey making themselves prominent.
Your eyes, fixed to your phone,
Have you noticed that I am here?
What is it that has amused you this much?

Your thumb,
Crooked as it lingers inches
Above the screen in your palm,
Enough surface area to cover the pill in your hand.

What is it with these drugs we now own?
They've got us constantly checking.
Fidgety.
Spending less time making eye contact with others,
Losing the opportunity to connect.

Mr Unknown.
With green eyes
Which barely dart across the carriage,
Instead are lifted to the map above heads,

You've barely managed to step off the train
Before your gaze left reality
Reality to your social realm.

The Underground

It's all about where,
Not how you sit.
It's all about who's opposite,
Not, next to you.
It's definitely about the story you see,
Not, the one you hear.

It's about the painted emotions
On the face of the owner
Who sits on the opposite side
In the same carriage as yourself
On the Jubilee Line to Stanmore.

It's about the lollipop
As round as the globe
Held by sticky fingers
Of the child, whose head
Rests in the lap of his mother
On the Circle Line to Ealing Broadway.

It's about the tiredness
Drawing him to the floor
For a quick power nap
Enough for an second wind
To take him home
On the Overground to West Croydon.

Remember,
There are times you need to stop.
Stop and spend time in the presence of others.
Stop and enjoy something different.
Stop and be.

- Careen Latoya -

Instigated Freestyle

It's the way they dart, seduction left behind as they dance. Less than longingly. Close to admiringly. Their moment, subtle, instigates actions as lips become pursed. Her eyes, they are professional, graceful and elegant. Perfect ballerinas.

He smiled at her but I can only assume she was either tired of guys hitting on her or she had such a messed up day, she wanted nothing to do with anyone else. She may have just wanted to get home. That had to be the only reason she looked at him in disgust.

That theory soon went flying through the doors of the train. Out came her phone and a smile. Happy to have received her message. Whatever was said to her from whomever was on the other side of her screen, lit her face up like a candle in darkness.

It's the way they dart, seduction left behind as they dance. Less than longingly. Close to admiringly. Their moment, subtle, instigates actions as lips become pursed. His eyes, they are professional, soft and peaceful. Perfect ballroom dancers.

He was tired. I can only imagine it was a long day for him. I wanted to say hi, but nerves got the best of me. I felt bad for her having been so rude to him. All he did was smile. Not asking for anything. It was courtesy. Tis a pity some are unaware of what it really is.

He wore a navy blue suit. I assumed he was in housing. He spoke properties to his colleague before we got on the train. His shirt was white with blue lines, running horizontally and vertically across his chocolate torso. His thick black glasses framed his rectangular face very well. His hands held elongated fingers, his left index finger tapping the back or his right. Not impatience, more, thought process.

Secret Souls

"You are handsome"
I want to say
"The sandy tinge of your locs,
Highlights the golden circular windows of your soul
And has unknowingly settled me."

Our eyes dance
Along lines of thread woven together
Encasing a body
Hidden from intruding minds.

Quenching ourselves,
We wish to slowly unwrap
Our forbidden fruit.

With actions this bold
We allow our eyes
To steal secret gazes
With hints of hope
Tapping away at our minds
Wishing to be see the spark,

Until another arises
And we brush them
In the crevices of our quintessence
Tucked away so they will not
Accidentally be unveiled.

No-one should be aware
Of our possibly wrong,
But perfectly right doings
Creating scenarios of
Relationships in our minds with strangers.

Mr. 181

I'd like to place pieces of you in various corners of my mind
But as it stands,
I may need to write your skin on my page.
A simple shade of handsome
With a subtle hue of two or more nations.

Your eyes; I wish I could spend this time delving into
What looks like brown, a shade that I'm unable to pen.
The bridge of your nose is a comforting slope.
Your lips, a perfect shade of pink
Accentuated by your reddish-brown strands.
You are a simple shade of handsome,
Alluringly endearing.
I've covered your physique in my thoughts;
An attractive fragrance every woman needs in a good man.

Mr. 181,
Did you feel my words crawling over your body
Replacing your tattoos?
This not so secret admiration note I've begun,
Could you tell from the smile across my lips?
Did my eyes give it all away?
As I stole a glance at you
When you walked towards home upon leaving me behind?
I'd like to see you again
Maybe at 9 another night as we wait in the cold?

I'd like to complete my penned painting of you.

My Stranger

Hello my stranger.
It was nice to reflectively meet you.

There's an image of you I am infatuated with.
It fades with time and this journey seems a little too short
For me to cling to the untouchable:
You.

Your eyes, I feel as though they search my soul
Though we are some seats apart.
Let me touch you my stranger.

Your shade.
The perfect touch of chocolate.
Dark.
Rich in antioxidants.
Breathable.
Perfect.

You are enjoyable from where I sit.
Seeing you there;
Admiring the mist of you prepared to disappear
Ready to become a figment of my imagination.

The tips of my fingers wish to slide across your face
To be massaged by your open follicles,
Graze across your lips,

Pink.

Close to the passionate red which ought to symbolise love.
I guess the minute you are with her,

Your lady,
The fire will spread deep within you,
Your lips now a nest of red beneath skin.

But, for now,
I will clasp your unpixilated image across my pages
Whispering my mind to you.

Why did you take a notebook from your bag
And a pen from the inner pocket of your coat?
Tell me stranger,
What is it that you are writing in your book?
Is it a funny story?
Or has it become
Two writers writing about each other
Using their reflection as they travel past midnight?

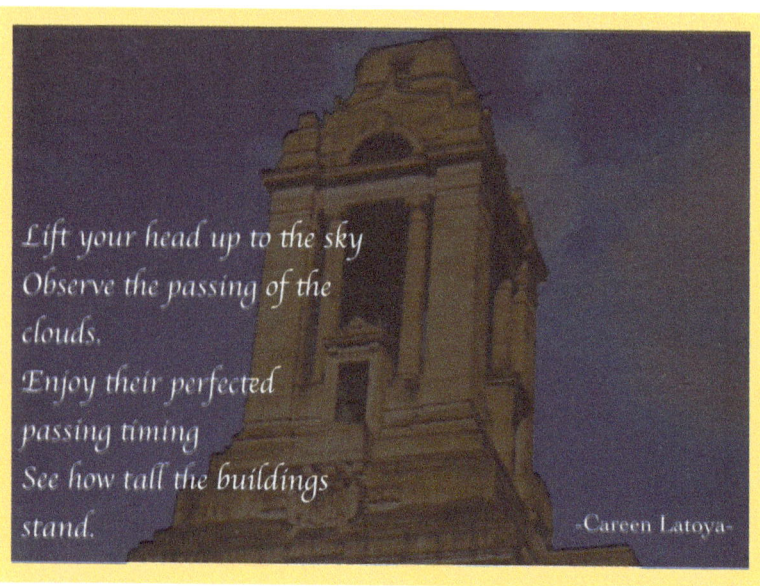

Lift your head up to the sky
Observe the passing of the clouds.
Enjoy their perfected passing timing
See how tall the buildings stand.

-Careen Latoya-

Mr. Jubilee Line

You scared me
Really scared me,
But I didn't know what to do
So forgive me.

I remember you clearly
Navy blue hooded jumper
With the hood fitting snuggly over your head
Comforting your unnerving thoughts.

You sat across from me,
Not directly...
But, ever so often I caught your eyes on me
Unaware that you needed someone to talk to.

You answered your phone
Sunk into your seat,
Ready for your palms to connect and rub at the fibres
Of your blue jeans accompanying your navy hoody.

You spoke,
Your words swiftly unravelled in my ears
Transported to my brain
Rocketed to my heart.
It was an express service.

Aim: Terrify Careen.
Mission: Successfully accomplished.

As I overheard you saying you wanted to kill yourself.

I shyly lifted my eyes to look into yours.
Deceptive
Echoing the eyes of a man with no worries
To be honest, you reminded me of the actor,
Derek Luke.

The way your...
I honestly don't know what to say
It was weird
I just wanted to sit next to you and talk.

But I was scared.
I considered your face.
Your eyes.
From which I constantly shifted my gaze.

Thinking about it now,
Your eyes were teary, yet
Your voice when you spoke, trickled with
deceptive confidence,
But, your eyes, they spoke a million sorrowful
words.

I was just scared to talk, well,
I didn't want you to know I was eavesdropping
But I wanted to get to know you
And I'm sorry for not stopping to talk to you.

You are still looking at me
I can see you
Your eyes fixed on me until discomfort sets in,
Breaking your gaze.

I should have told you how much life is worth
Find out your interests
Get to know you
And tell you, your current situation is only minor.

Your circumstances are a momentary truth
And it has been bothering me
That I wasn't able to talk to you
Even if it was only for a second.

I'm hoping one day we will be able to meet again
Hopefully then, I'd be able to tell you everything
that was on my mind
How attractive you are and one day someone
will be with you
Through the good and the bad.

Well, if not then, maybe now.
Life holds trials and surprises for us.
It shapes us into better and stronger individuals
It breaks our bad habits and characteristics.

It is more than you will ever guess
Just give it time to unfold
And sit back whilst you learn the lessons
It has to offer.

Danger

It's as though we know
Danger lies ahead
So choose to be away from it
That its arms may not reach out
When slumber is dismissed.

Our assumed danger
Is curled into a comforting position
Dirtied from today's adventure.
Arms tucked between knees
Praying not to be disturbed.

His face distantly visible
Soon to become
Another faded memory
Discussed on the other side of double doors
Avoided at all costs climbing through tunnels.

Rocking with the vibration
Of iron wheels
Against metallic tracks
Using the whirring and chugging
As his lullaby.

Hush-a-bye Danger
Curled 'cross three seats
Of the Circle Line's soft beat
Fanning at that which looms in a dream
Carved into the backdrop of tonight's grey fate.

Hey Mr Danger,
Do you have a place to lay your head
After being forced to peel your eyes open
At the end of the conductor's journey
To be asked to leave, before being forcibly removed?

Am I too quick to assume
This was the longest your eyes have been closed
To allow you to drift away,
Leaving the world's problems behind?
Escaping the inescapable by

Preserving the preservable.
Your life.
Which remains unknown to
The commuters of the night
Riding to their own treacherous dooms.

It's as though we know
Danger lies ahead
Tucked away in the soul
Of a sleeping body
Borrowing time to recharge for day number
Danger

It's as though we know
Danger lies ahead
So choose to be away from it
That its arms may not reach out
When slumber is dismissed.

Our assumed danger
Is curled into a comforting position
Dirtied from today's adventure.
Arms tucked between knees
Praying not to be disturbed.

His face distantly visible
Soon to become
Another faded memory
Discussed on the other side of double doors
Avoided at all costs climbing through tunnels.

Rocking with the vibration
Of iron wheels
Against metallic tracks
Using the whirring and chugging
As his lullaby.

Hush-a-bye Danger

Mr. Where is Home?

I've been told home is where the heart is
But no-one has ever mentioned the heart's location
And now we're fumbling to find two feet
Constantly on the move
Trying to settle down
But not willing to settle for anything.

Do we need to find someone to blame
For this constant pillar to post movement?
This loss of self,
Not knowing if the ledge on which we stand
Holds the foundation of our being.

Mr. Can you tell me where home is?
Are my roots the definition
Of the sense of self that I'm missing?
The whereabouts of my nature
Gone with the wind
But unable to be blown unless
Tight curls are straightened.
Is that where my home is?
What about you?
Do you reckon home dawdles
In the cracks of you history's pavement
African ancestors fighting to sit up in your tomb
Calling out for you to recognise their voice?
Are they
Lost between pages where words aren't extended
Missing pieces of a jigsaw puzzle
Which connects you to who you ought to be?

Was home buried six feet
Under when the head of your family
Was taken before the rest was ready
To take over and continue the legacy?

Mr. Can you tell me where home is?
I'd rather not have you lie to me.
Can you recreate it for me?
Show me what it once was for you
Or were you never acquainted with it?

How do I find where home is to be built
If the sole of my feet cannot ground themselves
Between the cracks I daily tread?
Mr.

Where is home when one loses their sense of identity?
Is it in the Christianity I've found myself in
Where spirituality is a secondary issue
Defining an essence of a being but carries no drip of continuity

When interests becomes confusion
Tell me where home is erected
For my heart is at times a shelter of my pain
Unable to sustain and maintain me.

Mr. Forgotten

Just a pinch of selfishness
To ensure we've forgotten
Those around wanting to be seen.
Those we walk past daily
But have paid no recognition to.

Hardly do we choose
To open our hearts,
To allow our minds to become
Hosts of empathy.
We live lies,
Continuously
Encouraging others to believe
We dacrifice self to become
"Symbols of kindness".

We've given this definition to
The homeless as we no longer
Have time to spare
To be able to stop for a second,
To listen to their stories,
To understand where they've come from.

Our impatience and quick judgement
Clouds our vision.
Killing us.

And as a small act of kindness gets ignored,
We allow a piece of us to die.
Desensitising us.
Removing our compassion.

Mr. Middle East

I will salute the media on your behalf.
Feet, shoulder width apart
Elbows bent,
Thumbs tucked in,
Index fingers to my forehead,
Hold, five seconds, no more.
I will salute the media on your behalf.

Your nation is criticised for the actions of the minority
So, you, a speck, are misrepresented by the killers.
The world has been taught to fear you
Driving you away with their stares.

I will salute the world with you.
Standing by your side
Shoulder to shoulder
Smiling.
With eyes filled with love
Turning to face you
Shaking right hands with each other,
Left elbows bent,
Left thumbs tucked in,
Index fingers on our brows,
Hold,
Twenty seconds
Give them a picture-perfect moment

The one they will never forget
But will never share,
Kept to themselves
As to never undo the propaganda.

Your bearded features being burnt into their minds.
Their images of you being reshaped.
A stamp of hope forming,
Your religion losing importance,
They now see you as a human.
I will salute the media with you.

If only the world would be more appreciative of you
Accepting you for who you are
And not the Islam they've created.
Let us be ironically iconic,
Allow me to salute the world with you.

Mr. Grey

The sweep of your silver strands
Numerous, with a black underlay peeping through.
The black hands of your glasses hugging your ears tightly
Enhancing your slender face.

I'm quite certain we have crossed paths before.
Your skin, thin and worn,
Years exaggerated but you
Keep your composure.

Sir, it is a pleasure to meet you
Though we are seated far apart

I'm content to have had the opportunity to see you again.

I rarely allow myself to escape
Into the world of acknowledgement
But with this opportunity,
I am grateful.

Your body,
Fragile.
Your back,
No longer with an upright spine.
But you continue with what needs to be done.

Your face is no home to complaints,
Your eyes, from a distance looks as the ocean does.

Peaceful.

I'm quite certain your wife enjoys being lost in them.
Green.
A reminder of the Earth's natural glow
That she would not question your love
As they closely resemble Mother Nature's.

Mr Poetry Luv

I think I may have forgotten
The eyes I so desperately tried to paint.
Life's stepped up,
You've been gone,
Our paths have yet to be crossed.

It was a night.
We spoke
Briefly
About a poem I wrote,
Performed,
Touching.
Moved on to books.
Mine.
His, your friend's.
You stopped talking.

But your eyes...
I've forgotten,
Did they hold passion?
Or were they filled with liquor?
I'm sure there was something,
Or was it the light from the darkness?

And your jawline,
Chiselled to perfection,
Symmetrical,
Psychology says this makes you more attractive,
I'd never beg to differ.
Nothing's disproportionate
It's pleasing to me.
But your eyes,
I think I've lost the way they felt on mine.

Moving towards your lips,
Your voice's entrance to the world,
How they looked?
That too has been forgotten.
Was it of no importance?
Or was I too wrapped up
Trying to capture the very nature of your eyes?

For days, I remembered your physique.
But months have trickled by,
Where time dripped into an ocean of
forgetfulness, And I've lost views of you,
What I thought
Was an unforgettable sight
Has now been lost.
Tangled in knots of others.

You've now become a face in the distance.

I,
You,
We've crossed paths once,
Strangers for a lifetime.

Mr Swag

Your style is captivating.
Enchanted me into a forest
Of wondering thoughts.

Our location the same
Yet your concerns are forties
And I'm worried about the end of my twenties.

You caught my eyes
Hooked me with your coordination
Trapped me with your skill.

I trust you, I think,
To place me unto the card
Which stores your memories.

I'd willingly be your model,
Superstarring my way
Into Alice's Wonderland
Wondering...

How many broken souls
Have you trapped
As they pretend their smile
Is a reflection of the way they feel?
Eyes peering into the depths of your lens
Hiding the vastness of reality's pain
Circumnavigating their way around the words
They have thought of to protect themselves.

They are their own version of anarchists
Fighting against the internal warfare they face
And this symbiosis between the lost and home
Cries loudest in the quietest possible way.

How many broken souls

Have you noticed standing before you
Hiding behind their sheepskins
Pretending to be in control?

Yet their control is lost in thought
And their blank stares shares stories
More haunting than paranormal activities
Seen clearly by connecting eyes.

Could your swag have distracted their thoughts
Washing away their doubts
That their brokenness thought it was fixed?

Your style.
Captivating.
Enchanted me into a forest
Of wondering thoughts.

You caught my eyes
The minute I saw you.
Hooked me with your coordination
Trapped me with your skill.

They all trusted you,
Hoping you could hide their pain
Masked behind Photoshop's layers
That their words would not be leaked from their lips.

No questions would be left unanswered
For their nakedness
Would be covered by your lenses.

Thank you for,
Swapping simple fabrics
Weaving wonderful lies
Accentuating appreciation of
Gratifying gratitude.

Your touch is possibly the only way
Models can show an air of bravery.
The more positive lies shared
The more comfortable they feel.

My Mind Her Body

For the first time
I've fallen in love with a masterpiece.
My heart opened up
And without a question or thought
Swallowed you into the pit of it
Savouring your continuously dripping
And ever so enthusiastic mind.

Your mind, an open space filled
With elongated metaphors
And screaming imageries
Along with the provocative
Rhyming trees which leaves me
Astounded.
I'm dumbfounded.

And my body has found it's resting place.
No longer am I hiding myself
For my barriers have fallen
At the drop of your mind.
My body has been lulled
Upon recognition that tonight
It's been graced with a time out card

Time out for thought
As consideration has carefully
Been placed on the table between us.
Yet the oceans between my sisters and I
Have somehow managed to sneak in.
Taking it upon itself
To pull me away from the soothing rhythms of you.

Now worry drowns the peace you created
Leaving me with a void
As I force myself to avoid recognising
The iron beaten truth.

For my sisters are being forced
To become uncomfortable with their femininity.
The monsters you managed to crush

Rebuild themselves stronger than before
Playing images of these men
Whom you do not resemble,
Destroying my sisters' self-value.
I find myself standing barefooted
Watching as their mothers attempt to protect them
Banging against their bodies

Preventing natural occurrences from occurring.
She can't physically afford to be
More than a flat chested babe
In hopes that she will not be seen as a woman
And won't need to marry too young
And minimising the risk
Of her being raped.

Shhhh...

Your mind puts me at ease once again.
I remember bodies are invisible to you,
My discomfort slips off
But my thoughts are still swinging
From the branches of my mind.
I see her,
Laying lifelessly on the dirt track

He dragged her to.
She is no longer a woman.
She has been misrepresented.
Like an unwanted object,
After he raped her soul
And stole her mentality
She was tossed aside.

Trusting you is something I want to do
But could you possibly see things through my heart?
Knowing that a woman can't be a woman
Because a man doesn't know how to be a man,
For he becomes governed by impoverished voices
Which doesn't make him a schizophrenic
But drags him down the path

Towards insanity of another sort.
This misconstrued ideology of why we were created
Has led to the degradation of us as women.
Our bodies are to create sweet sounding music
When love is made to us.
Instead, we shriek and howl once the pain drives through our bodies
As we are being forced to undergo the removal

Of our clitoris through clitoridectomy
Or undergo excision, just to remove our labia
Better yet, just to supposedly protect ourselves
From the likes of the wolves with no control
We endure the pain from infibulation
Just to narrow our vaginal opening,
Making us feel as though we must be ashamed to be a woman.

The men who are not you, have tormented us over the years,
Seen us as trophies to be collected for recognition
To say how many of us they slaughtered
Or how they managed to destroy us
And how good they felt taking control.

However,
Tonight you reminded me that not all men are
like this.
But what happens when we depart?
What happens to my sisters who are still being
told They are not allowed to get any bigger than an
A cup?
I've got it good
But what happens to them?
Where does your mind leave them?

Taxi Thugs

A rancid red mouldy justice
Is wrung from the hands of mothers
Whose daughters were wronged.

Trust vanishes from the pages
Where its meaning once paid bills
And is now buried on top of bodies

Of missing girls
Innocent and jeered
By the inability to put criminals away.

Her life was barely lived
Our justice system now mocked
By residents and visitors.

Bodies torn,
Ripped in places.
Souls stopped,

Hearts broken,
Gaining consolations worth nothing.
Slavery being repeated in an uncanny form

Lost identity
Handed to untaught men
Stealing lives, accumulating numbers

Yet years are subtracted
From the deserved sentences
In an ocean of blood.

The system fails to prevail
As joy caves in on itself
Questioning the safety of our women.
At the belief of some,
A woman on her period is dangerous
But they do not condemn the men who takes
advantages of women.

His *'power'* drags pain
Through the minds of the young, Unequally
wrestling the wrecked weak.

Uproar surges heavily
As the rush of a river
From a broken dam.

Clasped hands tighten their grip
Praying for help
But the culprits remain freely walking

No cuffs behind their backs
As the fabric of their taxis
Prepares itself to devour the next victim.

The Train Fella

He expected more than he deserved
Shaking the ground beneath my feet
Expecting me to stumble and back down
Because he thinks he is the one
He is the *'right one'*
All because he is **a man**.

What has gender got to do with this?
Why are gender roles still playing on his mind?
Why must he be like every other man out there
Who holds the belief in their minds
That a woman should be cooking their meals
And washing their dirty draws?

Why did he expect that I,
Upon having met him a day shy of a week ago
Would be cooking for him
Because he said so
And to make matters worse
He thinks that I should be doing this

Without that ring on my finger
Which would have only reached there
After some years of us being together
And me saying 'I do' at an altar.

He feels that I made an absurd
And utterly despicable statement
For I will not be playing wife without the ring.

He believes that a man should do hard labour
And the only labour a wife should do
Is to be at home with the kids, cook,
And clean and if she wants.
Yes, if she wants,
She is allowed to run her own **little** business.

He is fearful.
Scared there is a possibility,
I, as the woman, would do better than him
So attempted to sand me down
That I may feel I have no self-worth
And would settle for less than I have worked hard for.

He felt as though I am a new age woman
Who always wants a bite of the apple
And am easily led away.

But is it wrong to stand firm on my beliefs?
Am I not entitled to do as I please
As long as they are in line with the laws of this land?
Along with the laws given by God?

I would not like to strip a man of his masculinity
But please do not try
To confine my rights to your boxed mind.
I was doing just fine before you and your rules
Came into my life.
Do not feel as though my life is now all about you
You must understand that you now have
A small fraction of my heart
So please do not overstep your boundary.

A relationship is not about me being your maid
It is about me being next to you
Linking arms with you
And behind you when you need to be pushed
Just so you can make it through to the end
Even in your arms, as we face each other
Whilst we speak through our eyes
Just to remind each other that we still 'do'.

Black King

When you said you loved my aura,
I thought it was for the sake of finding words to be polite.
Even when you identified me for who I am,
I thought you were trying to show your level of consciousness
Being 'woke' with the rest.
I thought you were sleep talking
And I'm sorry.

I doubted the fact that
You know your identity;
With a clear understanding of where you belong
And the position you hold in society.
King, I thank you for replacing my ignorance with joy.

Your bars are uplifting,
But I know you are still being judged
And I'm sorry that you are drowning.
So if needs be, I will do whatever I can to help you
Because you deserve much more
Than the daggers you receive from your own black women.

Your ancestors walked miles, fought fights
Hunted, and protected,
Not for you to settle for less.

I'm sure by now you've identified your worth
Drawing on your strengths to be the king you are to be
Leading the weak from their shackles and chains.

Black King, continue.
Step up.

Remain awake.

You have the potential to be the world's greatest!
Do not prevent your own success.
Be the man you ought to be.

Do not live in the shadows of your fears.
Recognise that you are great,
With greatness to be achieved.

Black King,
You have an empire to rule
With people who will look up to you.

Black King,
Believe you can.
Go for it.

Black King,
Step up to the challenges life throws at you.
Work your way to the top.

Black King,
Be great.
Take charge.

I am happy you have seen the king in you
For that self recognition has opened your eyes
To the crown worn on my head

You see the Empress in me
And it melts my heart
When you call me by name.

Black King,
Your chocolate skin glows
With wisdom and courage
Never forget
To look into your own eyes
And remind you of your
worth

You are handsome.
You are a boss.
You are special.
You are a king.

Dear White Boy

I laughed internally as your legs dangled from your body
But your persistence was still admirable to me.

You held on for dear life
Your feet uncontrollably gasping for air.

I thought it brave of you,
Scrawny and untrained, working without a partner.

But that was three months ago
And I had to admit you were much better than I am.

As the new year, has opened its sleep filled eyes, A new you emerged.

Before me now sits a man, who persisted, Ignoring the sniggers of my mind.

And the awkward stares
I've exchanged with an unknowing you.

Dear White Boy,

Your transformation
Is an inspiration.
Proving persistence
To be the key to change
Growing at a rate
Some are unable to maintain.

You've done well
And look amazing.

With no guess game attached,
I do not wish to judge you
For your efforts are beyond questionable.
Valiant.

I need for you to
Refuse to answer any question
Pertaining to this new you
If a body wrongly interrogated, you.
You've shifted my gaze,
Curtaining my thoughts.
Seeing you has recentred hope.
Now I know,
If there was hope
For an untrained you,
An untrained me
With the correct mind
Set and focus
Will be as good as
You.

Sincerely,

Your Gym Buddy.

Mr. 8-8:40pm

        Out!
  In!   Out!
    Up!   In!
                      Up!

Surreptitiously repeated,
Muscles warm enough to draw necessities from the blood
As   Out!
     In!
       Up!
                Out!
              In!
                Up!

Is engulfed by the thickness of the musical blanket
We've become accustomed to.
Heart rates above the norm,
Bodies forcing sweat to hit
The mat on which we stand.
You charge that we push
                            Out!
                  Come
                    In!
                And jump
                    Up

No break,
Only a minute of
Pushing Out
Coming In
Jumping Up.
We tire in this time
And you continue to
Encouragingly engage us,
Getting us closer to goals.
All hunger fades

For focus is drawn to
          Out!
    In!
      Up!
          Out!
    In!
      Up!

Seek Ye First

I have been forced to drink their poison of insecurities,
Killing the bright yellow petals, I carefully formed.
I can see it wrapping its taut green weeds around my veins
Threatening to cut the supply from my empowered air
That I may fall into a bed of dependence
To run into the arms of a complacent accepted abuse.

I am being forced to find a confession booth
To utter the words "forgive me father for I have sinned
As I have not found the ribs to which I am to be connected
And the first three letters of my being have caused offence to my elders.
I am single and a curse, for it is not right that a 27-year-old be alone
With no man whom she can call her own."

But for my elders who project their fears onto me
I cannot speak for their understanding of self-appreciation.
I feel they are either enslaved by Christianity
Or misguided by their foremothers
And society's seeming definition of what it means to be happy.
Their happiness is lost in translation
Either, scraped at from the surface of their marriages

Or the relationships they tattoo over their skins.
Their eyes pour shame and pain over me
For I have not taken home the fruit they have all hoped for;
The attachment to a man, ignoring my need for self-appreciation.

But I'm grateful for my sisters for they have reminded me
That singleness is not to be condemned
Nor should I feel ashamed of my status
Though our elders have a misconstrued understanding
Of progressive steps in knowing one's self
Which knits together two individuals who can call themselves whole.

We may not have been taught to appreciate our time alone
But my sisters are aware of its eminent importance
Being able to get to grips with who we are
Without having to spend the time focussing on making him content
When we haven't been satisfied with ourselves enough
To offer the pieces which are missing and untouched.

Our singledom spells freedom and wholeness
Whether or not we are always secure within it
We are still grateful for the time to create and develop

Encasing ourselves into a cocoon as our wings are formed
So when the right he comes we can safely perch on his finger
Knowing he will cause no harm or allow harm to be caused.
Stop forcing me to drink your insecurities,

I rather drown in my sorrowful peace
With my yellow shining through
Than to be trapped in pain
With a man I can barely love
Because I was forced not to love myself

As you, my elders, find it shameful that I am still unwed.

App

Tinder's tender fingers
Swipes right-to-left, left-to-right
While Dory screams at us
Telling us to
Put the phone down
And get a life.

But electronics
Stole our lives
And now they are
Trapped on screens
In gigabytes, not enough to
Store our world.

And, the traditional way
To fall in love
Has been eradicated
For we are too busy
To spend time with family
Let alone to make time for a stranger

We create profiles
Well decorated to sell ourselves
To an audience
Whom we can blindly date
And choose the suitable fella
Who fits our agenda.

We look at attraction,
Get lost in the dreams on show
Testing the unseen hearts
Disregarding the worlds embedded beneath pictures
Hoping cupid will arrive.

Ain't it funny how
We expect to fall in
Superficial unexposed love
By looking at images
And words from
Someone we ain't never met?

We prefer to tell them
What we look like
If we have no picture on display
And hope.
Hearts in our mouths hoping
Our e-personality is good enough for them.

Tap-tap-tap-tapping away at our phones
Swiping left because, they
Do not meet our standards.
Swiping right because, this one,
Looks okay and no sign of
Attached craziness pops up.

The fear of never finding
The love of our life
Strangles our mind and
Forces us to blindly e-date
Trying to feel
A little comfort in our doings.

Then the horror love flicks we've seen
About the creepy guy sitting in a café
Suddenly refreshes in our mind
As we refresh the page
In a state
Buffering and contemplating.
Carrying desperation, wanting,

To be loved. But it's left us
Ready and willing to do anything
Except meeting him in town
For a quick trip to a coffee shop
The guide into his world.

Aint it funny how
We expect to fall in
Superficial unexposed love
By looking at images
And words from
Someone whom we've never met?

Scare to approach others.
The faces we see daily
Of the people we meet.
We fail to look into and dream
Of being with someone someday
Afraid of speaking to strangers in the flesh.

Absorbing the picture because it
Speaks a thousand words
And his represents a
Respectable and approachable guy
With impurities extracted
So we only see the good him
Which forces us to forget to ask about flaws.

The funny thing is,
It's in the back of our mind
That he is imperfect
And we want to know his blemishes
But have conveniently forget
That we too are no saint.

We forget to mention
That there is a possibility
We might be clingy
And will need to know
His constant whereabouts

So he should prepare himself.
A personality would be required
But we've hidden that
In a perfect description
Of who we want him to fall for But
we have the nerve
To want a 'real' man.

Ain't it funny how
We expect to fall in
Superficial unexpected love
By looking at images
And words from
Someone whom we've never met?

Why have our standards
Fallen in introvertedness
And we hide the real us
In fear that it will not be
Good enough
Though we crave honesty?

Tinder's tender fingers
Swipes right-to-left, left-to-right
While Dory screams at us Telling
us to
Put the phone down
And get a life.

Mr's Call Girl

He wanted me to be his call girl
After hours stargazing through the phone
Midnight entertainment
Nothing more than verbal engagement
It's a friend I was looking for.
Had me answering his calls
And sharing hours with him
But he still couldn't fit the bill
And I saw our time drawing to a close.
No more hours paid for in laughter,
He wanted me to be his call girl.

Calling when he needed
Nothing more than another voice
On the other end
Pretending to care,
He, fooled me.
I ranted and raved and vented to him,
And he played the fool very well
Unaided in his actions
He got me,
Down to crossing my t's and dotting my i's
He knew the deal.
Perfect communicator,
Mate,
He wanted me to be his call girl.

Willing to pay whenever I was in a bind
Laughing when the placard said so
So there I was waiting,
Hoping he'd pop the question

Not realising I was the joker in his castle
Just another one to waste time on
Because he had so much of it on his hands
He didn't know what to do with it.
This call girl outsmarted him
Managed to get through
With the help, he provided.
The queen in this joker started to shine
through No longer did she need to be paid
With his meagre time
Now standing on the platform
He unknowingly built for her.

He wanted me to be his call girl
But failed to see
This call girl's future was already
Written in the same stars we gazed at
As I wrote cheques to clear his debt
Getting him off my chest like a bad cold
As vile as phlegm
Needed to be hawked and coughed up
Clearing my sinuses
Preparing the way for a fresh start.

He wanted me to be this call girl
Who'd be willing to drop everything
Come round and cook for him
The minute he ordered a dish
But my chef was on vacation
Not willing to return unless my husband came
And he didn't seem to fit the description
Nor look the same as the man
On the wanted poster hanging above my head.

He wanted me to be his call girl
Genuine and honest
No nonsense kind of woman

One he could have a laugh with
Who I'm sure he called a fool
When talking to his boys
Which if it were the case,

I wouldn't be mad
All because he would have been right
But then and only then at that moment
For my senses have returned
And blinded I no longer am.

He wanted me...
ME!
He wanted me to be his call girl
After hours stargazing through the phone
Midnight entertainment
Nothing more than verbal engagement
It's a friend I was looking for
But I didn't stop to think
That friend would never be found
In anyone else but the original
Because knockoffs were fraudulent

He wanted me to be his fraud girl
After mindless hours on the phone
Midnight entertainment,
Discussions wanting to become arguments.
Silence.
Nothing more than petty verbal engagement
Sharing hours with him
Many I wish I could get back
But time has never been refundable
Nor up for exchange
I saw our time drawing to a close
And he called the shots
That last day we said goodbye
Because I was too strong for him

Standing my ground
Not the way he would have expected
So classed me as argumentative.
It was goodbye or change the subject

He no longer wanted me to be his call girl.
He found himself a permanent girl
Rebounded on the ex
Fulfilled his expectations on his tick list.
She met the standards he had never told me about
And bitterness only knocked my door to tell me
He'd be around for a more appropriate time
For this time round required a backbone to be erected
Not him, bitterness, to swallow me up
Or his friend pride, to hide me from the world,

A backbone to keep me upright
As I found myself in the world again.
He chose goodbye
And my subject changed to
Home-learning and self-taught
Learning more about me on a deeper level
Than I had ever exposed.

10 for Me

Love,
Can it be found in the confines of
A brown, worn, comforting leather armchair?
The armchair I wished would swallow me up
As I spoke to guy after guy after guy
Back to back to back,
Not one, not two, not three,
But Ten.
Ten different flavours of chocolate
Asking me to open up to them.

The extrovert in me was asleep,
Recharging for the week ahead
And my introvert sat on my lap
Blocking me from being the true me
And giving them a shell to be held.
I had put myself through a lot
All in the space of two hours and some change
Whilst the day-to-day me
Wanted to kick these boots off,
Slip my feet into trainers
And chill.

But instead,
I exposed myself to the speed,
Drugged my way into another world
Questioning what I set myself up for
Savouring the taste of a poem on my lips
As the experience, would surely work
With finding a start.

Quizzical eyes gazing into the depths of closed souls
As I forced myself to stop from disappearing
Into the dark ocean

Which consoled me
As the artificial heat lulled me into peacefulness.

Love,
Can it be found in 3 minutes of an open ring?
Each round being fought by different men.
Darling, is luck your lady tonight?

Nervousness danced across the staves of my heart
Demanding I left the fellow singles behind
As my one need was fulfilled
After 15 minutes
With 5 guys
And one me.
Ten flavours of chocolate to be indulged
And I successfully made it through 5.
I'm sure the other 4 would be okay
Because number 10 was late.
And he got the honest truth.
This game I played was too much for me
I was ready to call it quits.

Love, not being my motive,
Sat on their shoulders,
Winked and waved,
Knowing my heart was only beating
To bleed words from this pen,
Which has been releasing thoughts of them across pages.

When it was over
I found myself floating in the comfort of
My brown, worn, leathery oceanic armchair.
My back stroked the depths of solitude
As peace resonated within me
Cradling introversion so I could once again be at ease.

Mr. You

I

Your fingerprints impress themselves on the cool of my skin
The lightest shade of you caressing my dark
Sensitively travelling through time
As we gaze upon the stars.
Oh how numerous they are.

We shake the earth that lies beneath our feet
From laughter's volcanic eruptions
Trembling in a vacuum of pain
Which clings to our lungs pulling us into each other.
Closer into each other's atmosphere.

Dancing in lightyears
Unaverred tipsy love lingering
Between the fabric of our connection
Sauntering in our minds.

II

I dream of you...

But I'm still yet to see you.
An unfiltered, unconventional version of you.
I wait beneath the stars
Feeling your breath creeping down my neck
Carving love on my goose bumps as they appear.

I'm still yet to feel you
Standing next to me as the earth shakes.

Uncontrollably controlling gravity
For us to remain upright in each other's arms
As the moon whispers to us.

I'm still yet to hear you
Telling true tales of the future us
Where your heart isn't a hidden agenda
Allowing time to cure the pain we've been through
Sprouting love from the aromatic earth beneath our feet.

I'm still yet to smell you
As you enter our home with a fresh musk
Tickling the effervescent cilia of mine as, they
Dancingly wait for you to be close enough
That we can sweetly be entangled together.

I'm still yet to taste your love
As it leaks from your lips trickling into the
Streams of my heart to last forever
Forcing me to fall in love with you all over again.
I am here. Waiting.

III

I dream of you,

I have grown tired of dreaming of
Playing hopscotch with men who play darts
With tranquiliser filled tips and an aim to numb heart and brain
Concocted with lies, to be the board, top score
One hundred and eighty.

To be added to the count of countless bodies
Riddled with the why was I cheated on
Or the what did I do wrong
Machinations of love which could no longer live
Wanting to be freed, this caged bird can't sing.

Swing low sweet chariot won't let me ride,
So, Mr. You, when you ask Where Art Thou?
My answer has been in the rigged structure of my body
Standing beneath our stars
Waiting for the sweet escape from this blighted dream

I can't take the feeling that one day I'll be sucker punched
If I continue to dream of the ones I cannot be with
Trapped in a whirlpool to spiral out of control
Because my anxiety can't handle that
I'm socially inept as it stands.

So, I've cut down my list from one hundred to one
No room for error
Just the galaxy with arms wide opened
Our names in the universe, but you've not even noticed,
I am here.

IV

I dream of you,

But you are still yet to see me
Looking into the eyes of you,
The man whose rib I carry in my body
The umbilical cord to my lovers' heart
We are so near yet so far apart

You are still yet to feel me
Under the thin of your skin
As we try to make up for the time we lost
Reconnecting souls in seconds
Smiles spread broadly across our faces.

You are still yet to hear me
As I sing the songs you love to hate
While we stand around in the still of time
Feet planted on tiles
Which holds our secrets we've yet to share.

You are still yet to smell me,
Lavender fresh from essential oils
Taunting you, knowing it's your kryptonite.
Someone's falling asleep before the other at nights
Angry love, it's all fun and games.

You are yet to taste my love
As it leaks from my lips trickling into the
Streams of your heart to last forever
Forcing you to fall in love with me all over again.
I am here. Waiting.

V

I dream of you.

So, when you ask 'Where Art Thou'
Remember I am asleep.
Waiting.
To end this nightmare I've started
Wondering if truly, one day we will meet.

That the Big Bang Theory will apply to us
For a collision to take place
That one day wherever it is in the future,
You and I will reconnect
All five senses heightened.

When you ask 'Where Art Thou'
Do know,
I am still standing where you left me
As I count the stars to see how long
Just how long it would take for you to return.

I am here.
My love in blocks of five. Quintuplets.
Just like the pentagon houses we once drew as kids
A dot-to-dot
You are my star. My universe.

I dream of us

> *Dancing in lightyears*
> *Unaverred tipsy love lingering*
> *Between the fabric of our connection*
> *Sauntering in our minds.*

Mr Suleiman

Under the arms of loneliness
My brown skin sings broken love songs
Trying to find the right dress
Which would be appeasing to your sight
When we first meet.
My perfume, I hope will not be too sweet
But refreshing enough to tickle you
Hiding the quiver of my vocal
But I do hope you find me.
I too dream with 3D glasses
Hoping your touches
Will be projected unto my skin.
Please don't stop searching.
I'm here waiting to swim through your emotions.

You are the reason
I've never given myself to anyone.
Their life had never matched meanings and
Our thoughts never mirrored each other's.
It was all infatuation
And I can't wait for us to share love.
I've been certain that our paths
Have entangled us in circumstances
Working together, building forces.
I'm in a cacophony of terror
Facing myself in the mirror
Listening closely to your verses
As they hang above my head.
Studying my body
Wanting it to be as picturesque
As you'd have imagined.

Cupid once told me, he'd have us waiting
Until we are close to giving up
Before releasing his arrow.
I too am looking for the same thing
And will give you my time
So we can embrace each other's warmth.

I am caught in a web of lies
Waiting to be unrestrained by you
Because I too am needing someone to
love. I am dancing with the stars
Riding the storm clouds
Bruised, making my way to the rainbow
To prepare me for you.

We are a metaphoric symbol of love.
Drawn into a vacuum of our minds
Waiting for the one,
As love stays on the outskirts,
I too am waiting for you.

- Careen Latoya -

Friday's King

Today I learnt chivalry is not dead,
Just hidden in generations
Trapped in a new form of manliness.

You've respelled my errors
Undoing knots of wrongs
Framing the mindset which is missing
That I may slowly break my wall down.

Today I learnt chivalry is lost
Between two pairs of tracksuit;
One loosely hanging by a thread,
Restricting the movement of legs.

The other fastened in its place.
Accompanied by an upper body
Including the head. Covered with a hoody,
Weighing heavily, pushing eyes to the floor.

My soul, stumbled over the fallen rock
From the wall I built,
Not one that's political
But one I've used to teach me things.

Daily myriads of mirages
Altered from alter-egos on dais,
Climbing ladders over the years
Adding to complete the 'to-be-completed'.

And as we've trotted through swamps
I've dirtied myself in my thinking.
Dreaming in real-time. HD TV
Was the standard viewing I craved

Yet the dale offered raggedness.
The faded black and white binoculars
Handed to me, taught me
All I thought was right about them.

The ones who wear your famous
Skin in shades ranging from dark to light
From black to white
Crossing over to the mixed,

Seeping into those who view themselves
A different colour, a colour
Left in the box with waxed crayons
Accidentally overlooked by my ignorance.

I'm sorry.

My soul, stumbled over fallen rocks
From the wall I built,
For your words breathed
An important change to me.

Giving me a fresh sight
For me to see the modifications,
Shifting my views with your gentle breeze.
A new state of awareness entered me.

Today I learnt, chivalry is not dead. Just
hidden in generations
Trapped in a new form of manliness

You've respelled my errors
Undoing knots of wrongs
Framing the mindset which is missing
That I may slowly break my wall down.

Today I learnt chivalry is lost,
Between two pairs of tracksuit,
One loosely hanging by a thread,
Restricting the movement of legs.
The other fastened in its place.
Accompanied by an upper body
Including the head. Covered with a hoody,
Weighing heavily, pushing eyes to the
floor.

We are no longer connected.
And the powerful pyramid
Of wants, desires, requirements and needs
Cracks

Mr Please-Call-Me

Trust me to choose you,
The one with his elbows out
Defending himself whilst he sleeps
Endangering others,

Trust me to choose you,
A man of no voice
But a hooded being,
Head bowed, eyes closed
Back slouched,
And legs, the aisle's hurdles.

Trust me to choose you,
A man of many words
Held between the tips of your fingers
Soothingly caressing covers
In the smooth of your palms.

Trust me to choose you.
I did my best to reduce my size
In the cramped seating area
For you took over your seat
And mine, as well as the one to your left.

My eyes danced
Between your book and him
Darting across the aisle at them
In the hopes
No-one would think of me as crazy
Or borderline strange.

But the cover held me,
Shiny and smooth.
Pulling me in as a magnet would do.
But you sir,

Sleeping under the fluorescent light
Held life in your hands
Obscuring my knowledge

Trust me to choose you,
Tall dark knight,
Avid reader, I presumed
Before having confirmation allocated.

Trust me to choose to
Ask a perfect stranger -
Masking introvertedness -
With the bravery, of
"May I have a read of the blurb?"
As opportunity was presented
For you stirred and were awakened,
Placing the wealth of words into your pocket.

Trust me to get to
Talking at length
With a man on the train
Walking side by side
About the history of us.

I've learnt to believe
That knowledge is limitless
And can be gained
On the cusp of the morning.

Mr. Please call me.	Feed me with what you know
Tell me more.	For I want to be transformed
	Into a better version of me.

it was LOVE

The city sleeps as he reminisces:
the warmth from her house wraps him tightly,
the kitchen produces flavours for a lifetime,
it was LOVE which kept him returning.

Had she been able to see the future
would anything have been different?
Would she have been kinder
or would she have failed to care?

I doubt it would have been the latter
her heart was in the right place
and she took him in as her own son
though he was only to be a tenant.

His children became her grandchildren
that very first time they didn't know what to call her
and her senses informed her of this
so she said, 'call me mom'.

His wife became her daughter-in-law
and she with respect and gratitude
was happy to embrace the presence
of the woman who looked after her husband.

He was only to be a tenant
But her heart was in the right place
She treated him as her own
So her love kept him returning.

His family didn't celebrate Christmas
But he always bought her a card
Chocolates and flowers
Or a bottle of wine

What more could he give
To the woman who mothered him
When he first set foot into this strange land
With his wife and daughters in North London?

Gradually, she became poorly
Unable to move around as she once did,
Her body began to fail her
She wasn't as she was when they just met.

Then that Christmas came,
He didn't know it would have been the last.
Now he's been told
She may have less than a week to live.

Her Guyanese timbre as strong as their Jamaican tone,
a house of Islanders enjoying each others company becoming a unit in little to no time because she treated him as her own.
He visited her quite often
Just as his mother back in Jamaica
He spent hours with her

Always coming home with Guyanese dishes.
"My mom is dying",
Pierced his daughter's heart.

The elder of the two,
But she didn't know what to say or do.
It resonated within her for hours.
Now she sits and writes this piece, Reminiscing on her father's behalf

As the city sleeps.
I must visit her before she passes.
It's only right.
He will visit her before her last breath is drawn.
His wife will stand by his side.

His wife stood by his side.
He visited her before her last breath was drawn. It was only right.
I visited her before she passed.

Find Your Voice

Let me, find your voice for you

Because, right now,
This moment as I speak,
No one cares for you!
Let me...
Find it in the belly of your pain
This heart wrenching burden you bare
Let me...
Dig through and find that
Golden tongue
Laced with hurt
Covered in a bile of lies
Let me...
Wipe it down
And not douse it in bleach
That it may not be sparkly and attractive
For its rawness is what's tantalising.

Let me,
Charm the snake which sitteth upon thy tongue
That it too like the phoenix will rise
Shedding its skin that the suppressed cries from your gut
Will no longer linger beneath its belly
Which slithers around in your mouth
Taking away pieces of you

Now, let me, find your voice for you.

I take full ownership for you being a mute
So, I want to hold your murmurs in the palms of my hands
To free you from your empirical mindset
Set in years of domesticated abuse
I, take full ownership for you being a mute
So, I want to hold your murmurs in the palms of my hands
To free you from your empirical mindset
Set in years of domesticated abuse

Because you haven't even come to terms with
The funeral held for you when you entered this world
And your mother's tears were a mixture of confusion
She knew within herself that she would send you mixed signals
Mainly signaling that you should always stifle your own tears
Though she shed many for you.
She knew she would tell you to keep your head up
That your vulnerability will not shine through
Because a glimpse of hurt was to only be shown by females
And you would not be taken seriously if you ever shed a tear
Real men don't cry
And I am one of the reasons you are as fake as they get
A counterfeit artefact wanting to be treated right
Yet my voice has only ever been extended for women.

Now I want to take it all back
Women are always being fought for
But never have we stopped to put you before us.
They say behind every good man is a good woman
Yet we are no good for we force you to think
You are not allowed to cry
Nor are you allowed to be emotional
Nor are you allowed to speak
For these all correlate with being weak
And that role was already taken by women
And is not to be shared
But we are swift to say you need to learn to communicate
When we already took your voice box
And tucked it away.

So let me, find your voice for you!

I'm sorry you've had to believe you are soundless
That your words should only relay
'I love yous'
Or
'You are beautiful'
Or
'What's for dinner?'
Or

Whatever else we expect to roll off your tongue
Which doesn't include
'Today was difficult for me'
Or
'It's all too much'
Or
'This is what's bugging me'
I'm sorry we've led you to believe
That you are of no importance more than
To insert below navel lines

Or to reach what's on the top shelf
Or to show off that manly body
Sliding your identity over our skins
I'm sorry we've emasculated you
We undoubtedly took all power from you
We've been fighting for our rights
Leaving you unsure
Not sure if you should stand up for you
Because, maybe, it would come across as
You being ungrateful because
You already get the better pay
And you have the big jobs
And you are seen in society
So, you can never go through anything we've been through
How dare you open your mouth
To ask to be treated fairly
When we've stripped you of your humanness?

Let me be the one who takes on the role
To show you that I am no longer society
I no longer believe a man should hide the way he feels I no longer believe a man should not speak
I no longer believe a man should be sexualised
That us as ladies should drool over you

A man is nothing
when he loses the ability
to understand his strength,
though fragile his soul may be.
My love, do not allow them
to break your spirit for it is the shell which holds you together.

- Careen Latoya -

www.ingramcontent.com/pod-product-compliance
Lightning Source LLC
Chambersburg PA
CBHW061232070526
44584CB00030B/4096